ICONS

DWAYNE JOHNSON

BY KATHELEEN CONNORS

Enslow PUBLISHING

Please visit our website, www.enslow.com.
For a free color catalog of all our high-quality books, call toll free 1-800-398-2504 or fax 1-877-980-4454.

Library of Congress Cataloging-in-Publication Data

Names: Connors, Kathleen, author.
Title: Dwayne Johnson / Kathleen Connors.
Description: Buffalo, New York : Enslow Publishing, 2026. | Includes index.
Identifiers: LCCN 2025001089 (print) | LCCN 2025001090 (ebook) | ISBN 9781978544529 (library binding) | ISBN 9781978544512 (paperback) | ISBN 9781978544536 (ebook)
Subjects: LCSH: Johnson, Dwayne, 1972---Juvenile literature. | Wrestlers--United States--Biography--Juvenile literature. | Actors--United States--Biography--Juvenile literature. | LCGFT: Biographies.
Classification: LCC GV1196.J64 C66 2026 (print) | LCC GV1196.J64 (ebook) | DDC 796.812092 [B]--dc23/eng/20250113
LC record available at https://lccn.loc.gov/2025001089
LC ebook record available at https://lccn.loc.gov/2025001090

Published in 2026 by
Enslow Publishing
2544 Clinton Street
Buffalo, NY 14224

Designer: Tanya Dellaccio Keeney
Editor: Kristen Rajczak Nelson

Photo credits: Cover Tinseltown/Shutterstock.com; p. 5 Sipa USA/Alamy Images; p. 7 Kathy Hutchins/Shutterstock.com; p. 9 ZUMA Press, Inc./Alamy Images; pp. 11, 14 Gavin Rodgers/Alamy Images; p. 13 MediaPunch Inc/Alamy Images; p. 15 Featureflash Photo Agency/Shutterstock.com; pp. 17, 19 Cinematic/Alamy Images; pp. 21 PA Images/Alamy Images; p. 23 Fred Duval/Shutterstock.com; p. 24 Barry King/Alamy Images; p. 25 BFA/Alamy Images; p. 27 Hyperstar/Alamy Images; p. 29 UPI/Alamy Images.

Printed in the United States of America

CPSIA compliance information: Batch #CSENS26: For further information contact Enslow Publishing, at 1-800-398-2504.

Contents

Words in the glossary appear in **bold** the first time they are used in the text.

At the Top

Dwayne Johnson is truly an **icon**. He's one of the highest-paid actors around today. His many fans see everything he does. Some have even wanted him to run for president! Dwayne worked hard to get to the top—and works even harder to stay there.

ICONIC!

In 2024, Dwayne held two Guinness World Records: most followed actor on TikTok and most followed American man in the world.

All in the Family

Dwayne was born on May 2, 1972, in California. His dad, Rocky Johnson, worked as a **professional wrestler**. His mom's name is Ata. Her father was a wrestler too! The family didn't have much money while Dwayne was growing up.

ICONIC!

Dwayne grew up all over the United States, including in Hawaii. His family often followed his dad's pro wrestling jobs.

Football Star?

Dwayne got into a lot of trouble when he was young. He would steal things he wanted. Then his family moved to Pennsylvania. Playing football in high school helped him get his act together. Dwayne went on to play for the University of Miami.

ICONIC!

Dwayne played defensive tackle at Miami. But, a hurt shoulder early on made him mostly a backup player on the team.

Dwayne wanted to play professional football. But, at just 22, Dwayne got cut from his team in the Candian Football League (CFL). He told his dad he wanted to learn the family business. He began wrestling for the World Wrestling Federation (WWF) in 1996.

ICONIC!

Dwayne says that after being cut by the CFL's Calgary Stampeders in 1995, he only had $7 left in his wallet.

THE
PEOPLES
EYEBROW

All the Way to WrestleMania

At first, Dwayne first went by the name Rocky Maivia. He truly became a star once he became a **heel** calling himself The Rock! He **performed** in the main event of WrestleMania XV in 1999 against wrestling great Stone Cold Steve Austin.

ICONIC!

As The Rock, Dwayne was in the main event at WrestleMania in 2000 and 2001 too. In 2002, he faced Hulk Hogan in a WrestleMania match called "Icon vs. Icon."

Looking Beyond the Ring

By the early 2000s, Dwayne was one of the biggest stars in the WWF, which became World Wrestling Entertainment (WWE) in 2002. His on-mic skills were second to none, with **catch phrases** reaching beyond wrestling fans. But Dwayne also wanted to act in movies!

ICONIC!

The Rock became known for being able to raise his eyebrow really high. He called this the "people's eyebrow."

Dwayne appeared as the Scorpion King in *The Mummy Returns* in 2001 and *The Scorpion King* in 2002. In 2004, his contract, or deal, with the WWE ended. He partly chose to step away from the ring to give a **career** in acting a real chance.

ICONIC!

*Years later, Dwayne said he left wrestling in 2004 because he wanted to be a worldwide success: "I wanted global **influence** in a very, very real and powerful way."*

Movie Star

Dwayne appeared in many family movies like *The Game Plan* and *Tooth Fairy.* Then, in 2011, his biggest **role** yet came as Luke Hobbs in *Fast Five.* Dwayne became an action star! He went on to star in the movies *Pain & Gain, San Andreas,* and others.

ICONIC!

*In movies, Dwayne has been **credited** as The Rock and Dwayne "The Rock" Johnson, as well as just Dwayne Johnson.*

Iconic Voice

Dwayne took on another iconic role in 2016. He performed the voice of Maui in the Disney movie *Moana*. Dwayne did his own singing as Maui. He practiced a lot to get the song "You're Welcome" just right.

ICONIC!

Dwayne voiced Maui again in Moana 2*, which came out in 2024. He also did the voice for Krypto in the movie* DC League of Super-Pets.

Success!

Dwayne began moving into another kind of acting around this time: **comedy**! *Central Intelligence* and *Baywatch* showed his silly side. *Jumanji: Welcome to the Jungle* came out in 2017. The comedy became one of Dwayne's biggest successes!

ICONIC!

Dwayne is about 6 feet 4 inches (1.9 m) tall and looks very strong. His size is often a part of his comedy!

Dwayne has continued to make hit movies! He starred in both *Jumanji: The Next Level* and the spin-off movie, *Fast & Furious Presents: Hobbs & Shaw* in 2019. Then, in 2021 Dwayne got to play an FBI agent in *Red Notice*.

ICONIC!

Dwayne has been on TV too. He starred in the show Ballers *and hosted* The Titan Games.

Back to the Ring

Dwayne hasn't left pro wrestling behind him for good. Over the years, he has come back to the WWE to perform with some of the biggest names in wrestling: John Cena, CM Punk, and, in 2024, Cody Rhodes and Seth Rollins.

ICONIC!

Dwayne has three daughters: Simone, Jasmine, and Tiana. Simone is now a professional wrestler like her dad!

RED NOTICE
NETFLIX

Business Icon

Dwayne co-founded a company called Seven Bucks Productions that makes TV shows, movies, and more. He also works with the clothing company Under Armour to make Project Rock gear. How much more will this icon accomplish?

ICONIC!

The TV show Young Rock *told the story of Dwayne's early life. He played himself on it!*

Timeline

1972	*Dwayne Johnson is born on May 2.*
1996	*He begins wrestling for the WWF (later WWE).*
1999-2001	*He performs in the main event of WrestleMania.*
2001	*He is in his first movie,* The Mummy Returns.
2011	*He appears as Luke Hobbs for the first time in* Fast Five.
2016	Moana *comes out.*
2017	Jumanji: Welcome to the Jungle *comes out.*
2019	Jumanji: The Next Level *and* Fast & Furious Presents: Hobbs & Shaw *come out.*
2021	Red Notice *comes out.*
2024	*Dwayne performs at WrestleMania XL.* Moana 2 *comes out.*

For More Information

BOOKS

Shuch, Mari C. *What You Never Knew About Dwayne Johnson*. Oxford, UK: Raintree, 2024.

Smith, Elliott. *Steve Austin vs. Dwayne Johnson: Wrestling Legends Face Off*. North Mankato, MN: Capstone Press, 2025.

WEBSITE

Dwayne "The Rock" Johnson

https://www.wwe.com/superstars/the-rock

Check out Dwayne's WWE profile here.

Seven Bucks Productions

https://sevenbucks.com/

Find out what's new for Dwayne's production company on this website.

Publisher's note to educators and parents: Our editors have carefully reviewed these websites to ensure that they are suitable for students. Many websites change frequently, however, and we cannot guarantee that a site's future contents will continue to meet our high standards of quality and educational value. Be advised that students should be closely supervised whenever they access the internet.

Glossary

career: The job someone chooses to do for a long time.

catch phrase: Something short a person is known for saying.

comedy: A movie, play, or book meant to make people laugh.

credit: To list by name a person who was part of making a movie or other media.

heel: In wrestling terms, the bad guy.

icon: A person who is very successful and admired.

influence: To have an effect on.

perform: To carry out an action in order to entertain.

professional wrestler: An athlete that performs a planned wrestling match meant to entertain.

role: The part a person plays.

Index